Crafts for Kids Who Are Wild About

Insects

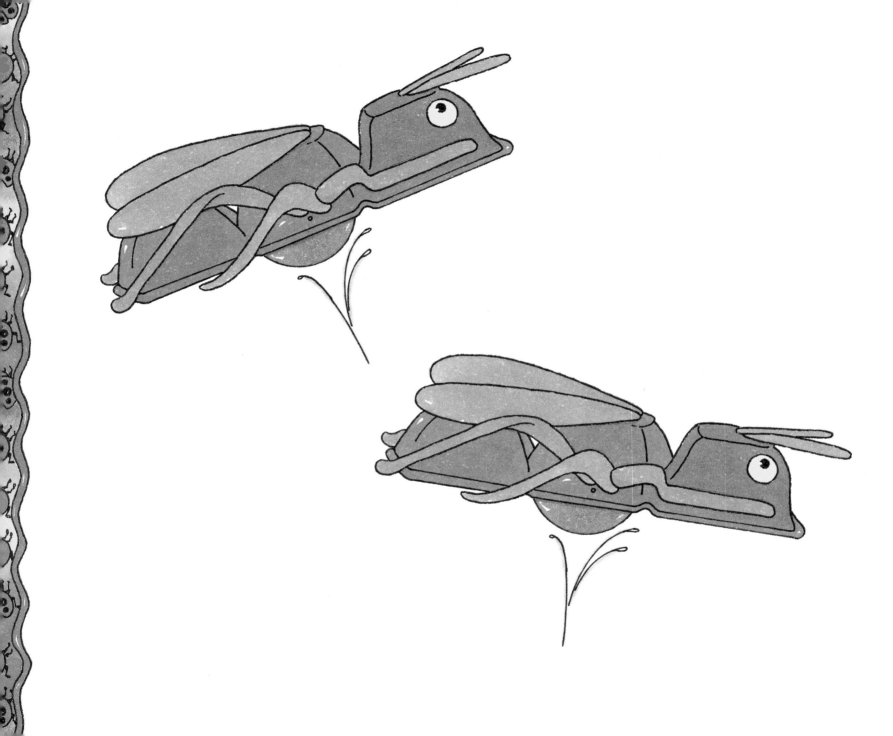

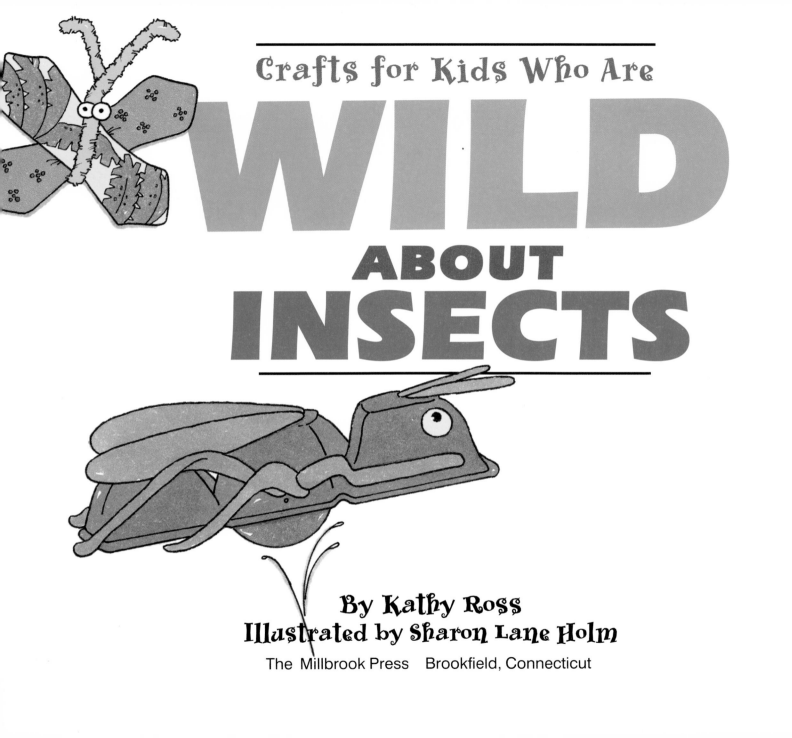

Crafts for Kids Who Are

WILD

ABOUT
INSECTS

By Kathy Ross
Illustrated by Sharon Lane Holm

The Millbrook Press   Brookfield, Connecticut

For my dear and wonderful friend, Beverly—K.R.
For my little brother, who always was a pest—S.L.H.

Library of Congress Cataloging-in-Publication Data
Ross, Kathy (Katharine Reynolds), 1948–
Crafts for kids who are wild about insects / Kathy Ross; illustrated by Sharon Lane Holm.
p. cm.
Includes bibliographical references.
Summary: Introduces the world of crawling and flying insects through twenty simple craft
projects.
ISBN 0-7613-0116-X (lib. bdg.)   ISBN 0-7613-0276-X (pbk.)
1. Handicrafts—Juvenile literature. 2. Insects in art—Juvenile literature. [1. Handicraft. 2.
Insects in art.] I. Holm, Sharon Lane, ill. II. Title.
TT160.R714217   1997
745.5—dc20   96-35801   CIP   AC

Published by The Millbrook Press, Inc.
2 Old New Milford Road
Brookfield, Connecticut 06804
//www.neca.comm/mall/millbrook

Contents

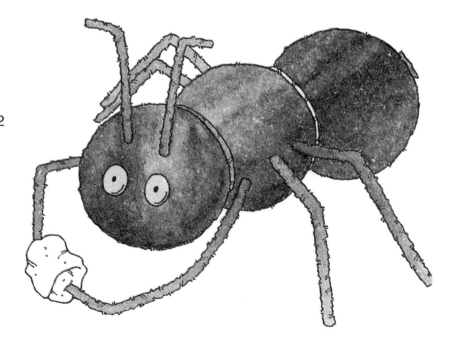

Introduction 7

Magnified Bugs 8

Lucky Ladybug Necklace 10

Butterfly Metamorphosis 12

Walkingstick 15

Caterpillar-to-Butterfly Puppet 16

Butterfly Lapel Pin 18

Paper Caterpillar to Butterfly 20

Flower and Bumblebee Face Mask 22

Flashing Firefly Puppet 24

Queen Wasp and Chambers 26

Hungry Mosquito 28

Jumping Grasshopper 30

Dog and Flea Game 32

Moth and Candle Stabile 34

Hunting Dragonfly 36

Worker Ant 38

Ants on a Picnic Basket Necklace 40
Venus's-flytrap and Fly Puppets 42
Scurrying Cockroach 44
Bug in the Grass Terrarium 46
Books About Insects 48

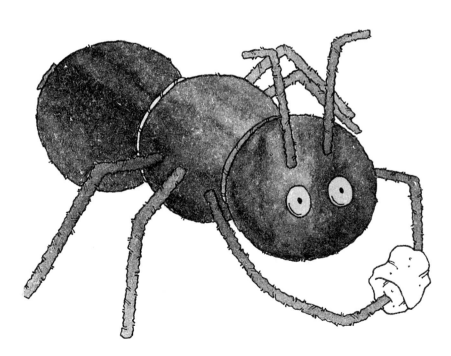

Introduction

All the creatures that I have included in this book are true insects. They meet the definition of an insect: three main body parts—a head, a thorax, and an abdomen; antennae on top of the head; six legs; and an outer shell that protects the soft insides. Many insects have compound eyes, meaning they have many lenses in each eye instead of just one. I have not added compound eyes on all of the models, but you may want to for the sake of accuracy.

Insects are fascinating creatures. What I have tried to do in this book is to feature one interesting trait for each insect I made. I had a lot of fun creating these insects, and I hope you will too.

Kathy Ross

Magnified Bugs

Here is what you need:

two small paper plates
plastic wrap
craft stick
masking tape
stapler
sharp black marker
black ink pad
black poster paint and a paintbrush
scissors
yarn in the color of your choice
white glue
newspaper to work on

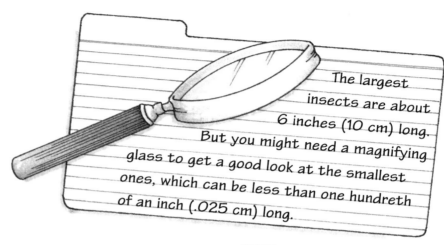

The largest insects are about 6 inches (10 cm) long. But you might need a magnifying glass to get a good look at the smallest ones, which can be less than one hundreth of an inch (.025 cm) long.

Here is what you do:

Cut the center out of one paper plate. Turn the remaining rim over and paint it black. Let it dry.

Turn the second plate eating side up. Press your finger on the ink pad and use ink fingerprints to make the three segments of an insect on the center of the plate. Draw in details of the insect with the black marker.

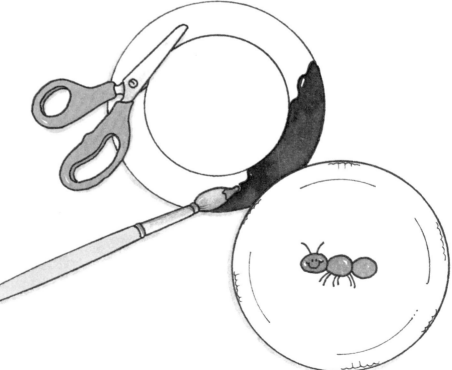

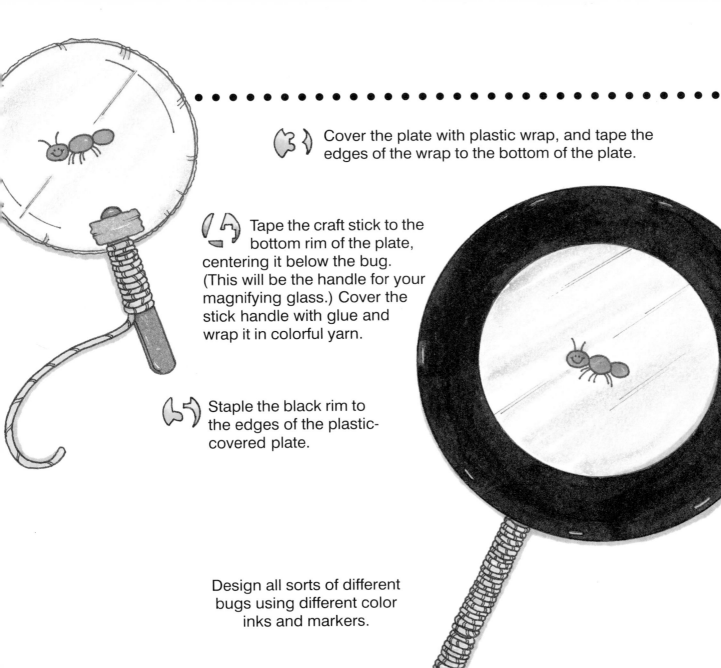

Cover the plate with plastic wrap, and tape the edges of the wrap to the bottom of the plate.

Tape the craft stick to the bottom rim of the plate, centering it below the bug. (This will be the handle for your magnifying glass.) Cover the stick handle with glue and wrap it in colorful yarn.

Staple the black rim to the edges of the plastic-covered plate.

Design all sorts of different bugs using different color inks and markers.

Lucky Ladybug Necklace

Here is what you need:

two pry-off bottle caps
red nail polish
sharp black permanent marker
black felt scrap
black yarn
scissors
white glue
a lucky penny

Some people say that ladybugs bring good luck. Maybe it is because they eat insects that are harmful to crops and gardens.

Here is what you do:

 Paint the outside of both bottle caps with red nail polish and let the polish dry.

Cut a small strip of black felt. Glue one end inside each cap to form a hinge that will allow the caps to open and close, forming a locket.

Cut a circle of black felt to fit inside one of the caps and glue it in place.

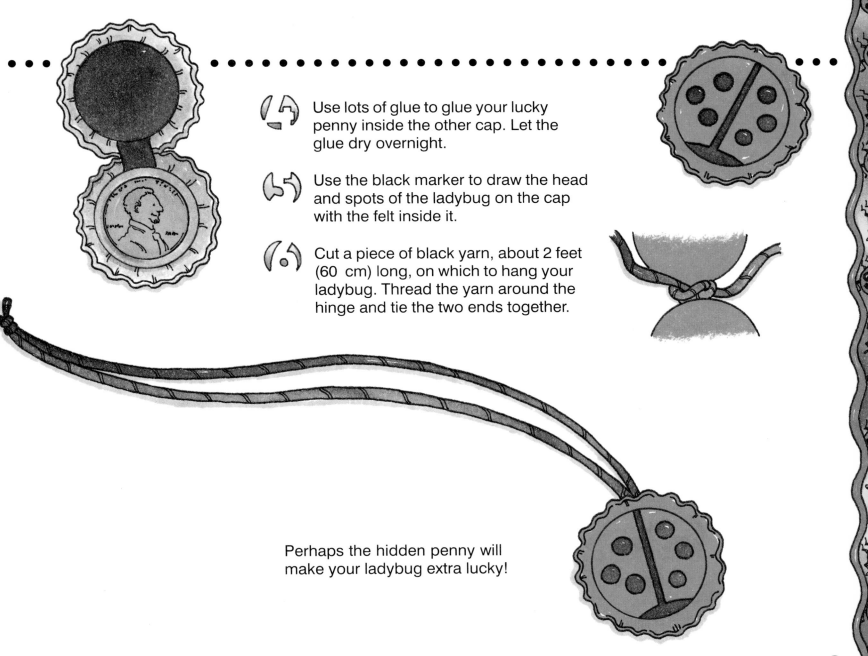

4. Use lots of glue to glue your lucky penny inside the other cap. Let the glue dry overnight.

5. Use the black marker to draw the head and spots of the ladybug on the cap with the felt inside it.

6. Cut a piece of black yarn, about 2 feet (60 cm) long, on which to hang your ladybug. Thread the yarn around the hinge and tie the two ends together.

Perhaps the hidden penny will make your ladybug extra lucky!

Butterfly Metamorphosis

Here is what you need:

cardboard egg carton
brown and blue poster paint
    plus other bright colors
paintbrush
hole punch
scissors
green yarn
green construction paper scrap
green pipe cleaner
popcorn kernel
spinach spiral pasta
shell-shaped pasta
bow-shaped pasta
four tiny wiggle eyes
piece of twig
white glue
Styrofoam tray for drying

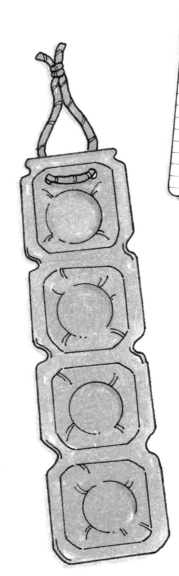

The butterfly goes through four different stages as it changes into an adult insect.

Here is what you do:

1) Cut four attached cups in a row from the egg carton.

2) Paint the front and back of the cups blue, and let them dry on the Styrofoam tray.

3) Stand the cups upright and punch two holes in the top of the top cup. Tie a piece of green yarn through the two holes and tie the ends together to form a hanger.

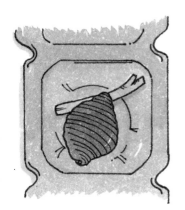

4 Cut a leaf shape from green paper to fit in the top cup. Glue the leaf in the cup, then glue a popcorn kernel on the leaf for an egg.

5 Glue some bits of green yarn in the second cup for grass. Glue the green spiral pasta on the grass for a caterpillar. Glue two tiny wiggle eyes at one end of the caterpillar.

6 Paint the shell-shaped pasta brown and let it dry. Glue the piece of twig in the third cup with the brown shell pasta hanging off it to look like a chrysalis.

7 Paint the bow-shaped pasta one or more bright colors.

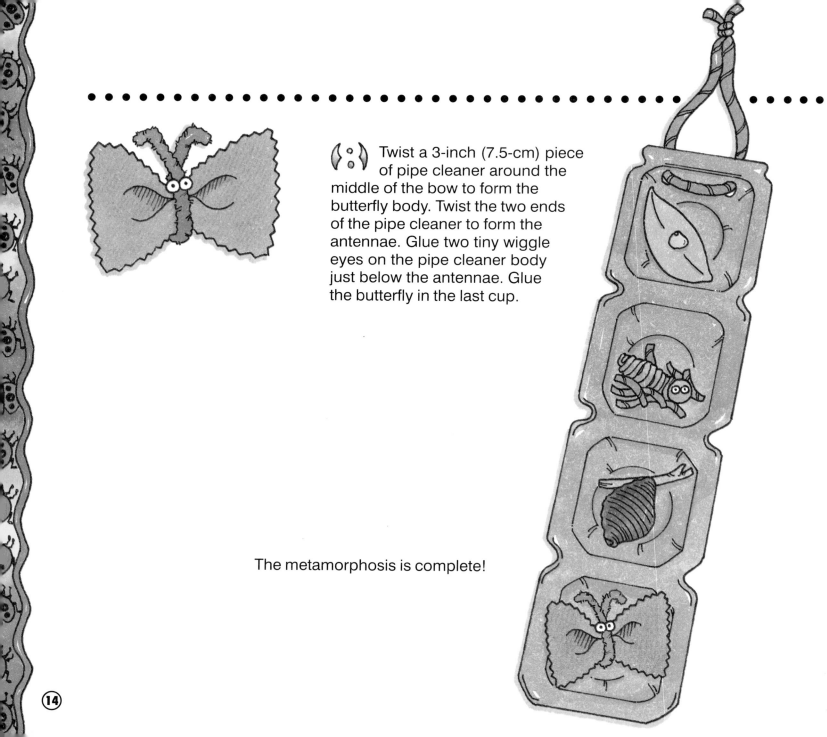

Twist a 3-inch (7.5-cm) piece of pipe cleaner around the middle of the bow to form the butterfly body. Twist the two ends of the pipe cleaner to form the antennae. Glue two tiny wiggle eyes on the pipe cleaner body just below the antennae. Glue the butterfly in the last cup.

The metamorphosis is complete!

Walkingstick

Here is what you need:

forked twig
two 12-inch (30-cm) black or brown pipe cleaners
two tiny wiggle eyes
brown poster paint and a paintbrush
scissors
white glue

Walkingsticks are hard to spot because they look so much like twigs that they blend right into the trees on which they live.

Here is what you do:

Trim a thin forked twig so that each of the forks is 1 inch (2.5 cm) long and the main stem is about 5 inches (12.5 cm) long. The twig will be the body of the insect, and the two forked pieces the antennae.

Cut three 6-inch (15-cm) pieces of black pipe cleaner for the legs. Wrap the center of each piece around the twig and bend the ends so that the insect will stand.

Brush some brown paint over the twig and the pipe cleaners to blend them together.

Glue the two wiggle eyes on each side of the antennae.

Set your walkingstick down on a low tree branch and challenge a friend to find it. Watch out for real walkingsticks, though. If this insect senses danger it sprays a foul-smelling liquid.

Caterpillar-to-Butterfly Puppet

Here is what you need:

two pairs of colored or patterned shoulder pads
two old adult sport socks with colored stripes
adult-size brown sock
1-inch (2.5-cm) safety pin
yellow paper scrap
black marker
scissors
white glue

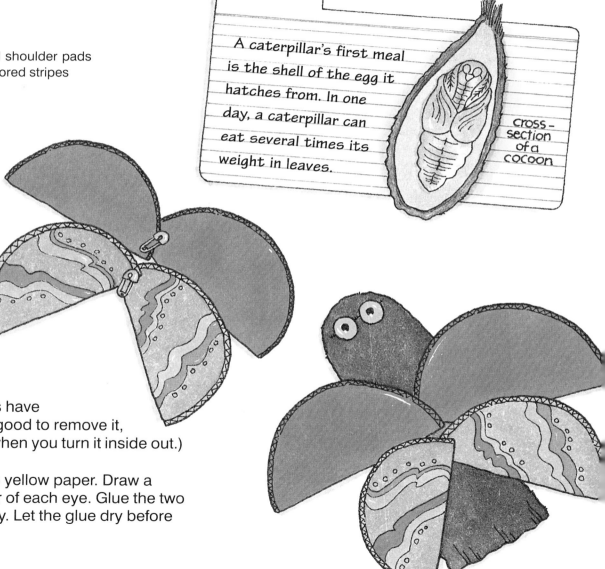

A caterpillar's first meal is the shell of the egg it hatches from. In one day, a caterpillar can eat several times its weight in leaves.

cross-section of a cocoon

Here is what you do:

Arrange the four shoulder pads into two separate sets of butterfly wings. Pin one set just behind the other on the bottom of the foot of the brown sock, about halfway between the heel and the toe. (If the shoulder pads have Velcro on them, it would be good to remove it, so it won't stick to the sock when you turn it inside out.)

Cut two eyes from the yellow paper. Draw a black dot in the center of each eye. Glue the two eyes to the top of the butterfly. Let the glue dry before continuing.

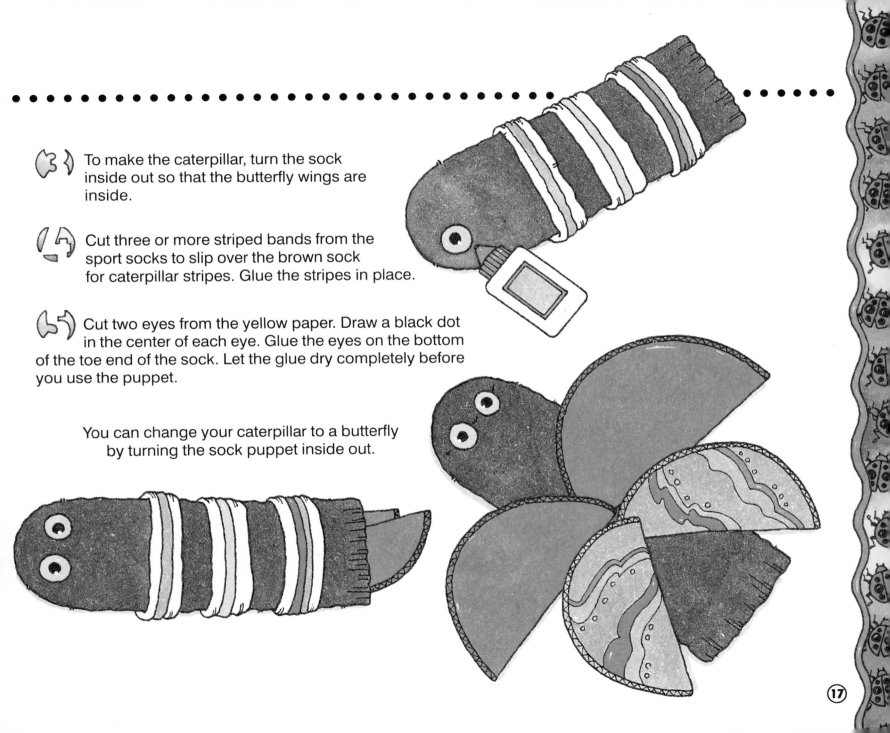

To make the caterpillar, turn the sock inside out so that the butterfly wings are inside.

Cut three or more striped bands from the sport socks to slip over the brown sock for caterpillar stripes. Glue the stripes in place.

Cut two eyes from the yellow paper. Draw a black dot in the center of each eye. Glue the eyes on the bottom of the toe end of the sock. Let the glue dry completely before you use the puppet.

You can change your caterpillar to a butterfly by turning the sock puppet inside out.

Butterfly Lapel Pin

Here is what you need:

two colorful old neckties
orange or yellow pipe cleaner
two tiny wiggle eyes
white glue
scissors
safety pin

When a butterfly hatches, it must pump liquid into its wings to make them expand.

Here is what you do:

Cut a 4-inch (10-cm) piece from the narrow end of each necktie, measuring from the tip of the point. Cut the flat end of each piece into a point to match the sewn point of the tie.

Set one piece over the other piece to form an X-shape with both cut points at the bottom.

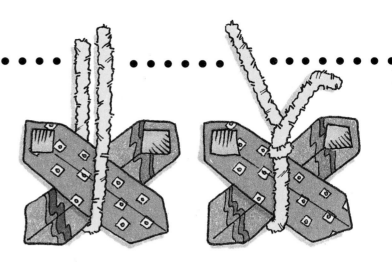

Cut a 6-inch (15-cm) piece of pipe cleaner. Fold the pipe cleaner in half over the center of the X so that the pipe cleaner forms the body of the butterfly and the tie pieces form the wings. Pinch the center of the wings together slightly, then wrap the two ends of the pipe cleaner around each other to form the antennae of the butterfly.

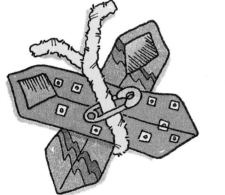

Glue two tiny wiggle eyes below the antennae.

Slide the safety pin through the back of the pipe cleaner body and the butterfly is ready to wear.

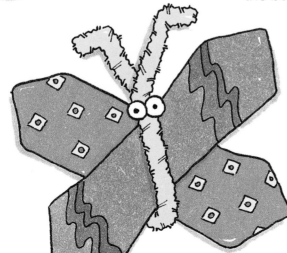

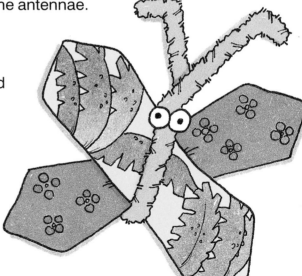

Paper Caterpillar to Butterfly

Here is what you need:

12-inch (30-cm) by 18-inch (46-cm) piece of
    construction paper in a bright color
markers or crayons
scissors

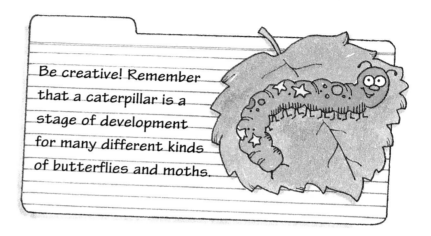

Be creative! Remember
that a caterpillar is a
stage of development
for many different kinds
of butterflies and moths.

Here is what you do:

Fold the construction paper in half so that you have a piece of paper that is 9 inches (23 cm) by 12 inches (30 cm). Sketch an arched caterpillar shape with the back of the caterpillar on the fold. Make the caterpillar as large as the paper will allow.

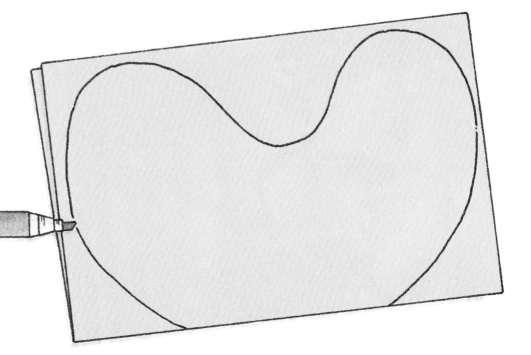

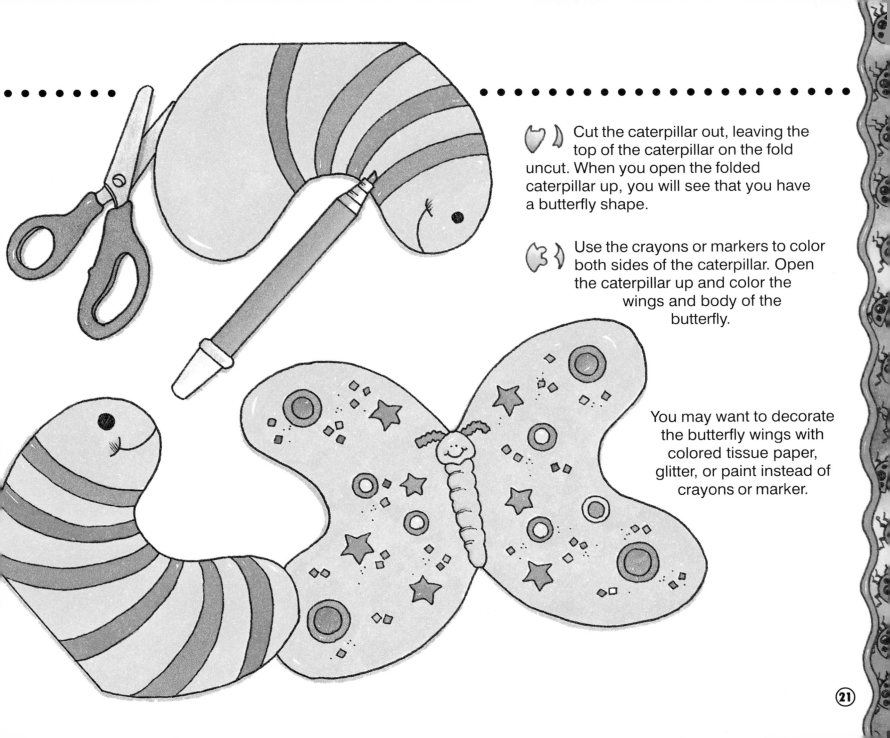

Cut the caterpillar out, leaving the top of the caterpillar on the fold uncut. When you open the folded caterpillar up, you will see that you have a butterfly shape.

Use the crayons or markers to color both sides of the caterpillar. Open the caterpillar up and color the wings and body of the butterfly.

You may want to decorate the butterfly wings with colored tissue paper, glitter, or paint instead of crayons or marker.

21

Flower and Bumblebee Face Mask

Here is what you need:

construction paper in a bright color
9-inch (23-cm) paper plate
12-inch (30-cm) pipe cleaners in yellow and black
cellophane tape
two tiny wiggle eyes
white glue
stapler
scissors

Bumblebees drink nectar from flowers.

Here is what you do:

Cut the center out of the paper plate.

Cut flower petals from the construction paper and glue them around the bottom side (the side that you do not eat on) of the plate frame. (If you want your flower to be very fancy, you could glue a little glitter on the petals.)

Cut a band from the construction paper. Fold the ends of the band inward and staple them to the top side of the plate frame. The band should fit around your head snugly enough to hold the flower mask in place.

To make the bee, hold the yellow and black pipe cleaners together. Starting at one end, wrap the pipe cleaners around your finger about four times. Bend the remaining length of the yellow pipe cleaner straight down. Wrap the black pipe cleaner around one of the ends of the spiral one more time to form a black head for the bee. Cut off the remaining black pipe cleaner.

Glue two tiny wiggle eyes to the head of the bee.

To make two sets of wings for the bee, fold four 2-inch (5-cm) pieces of tape in half with the sticky sides together. Cut a little wing out of each piece. Tuck the wings in between the pipe cleaners on the back of the bee and rub some glue over the pipe cleaners to hold the wings in place.

Staple the end of the yellow pipe cleaner to the top back of the flower so that the bee wiggles back and forth above the flower.

You and your friends can make a whole garden—but watch out for real bees!

Flashing Firefly Puppet

Here is what you need:

adult-size brown sock with 8 to 9 inches (20 to 23 cm) of ribbing
two brown buttons
four 12-inch (30-cm) orange pipe cleaners
white tissue paper
white glue
scissors
green see-through disposable plastic cup
flashlight
rubber band

Fireflies flash to each other with their lights.

Here is what you do:

Cut the foot off the sock. The ribbed part will be the body of the firefly.

Put the top of the sock over the rim of the cup. Hold the cup in place with a rubber band. Fold about 1 inch (2.5 cm) of the top of the sock over the rubber band to conceal it.

Glue two brown buttons on one side of the other end of the sock for the eyes.

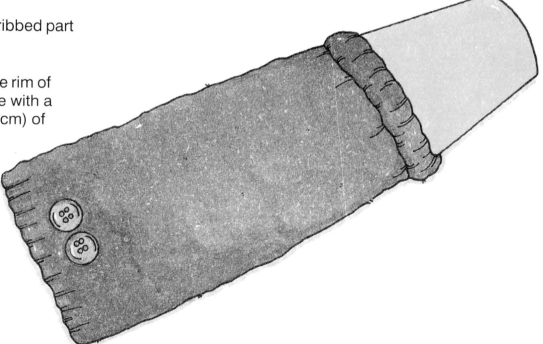

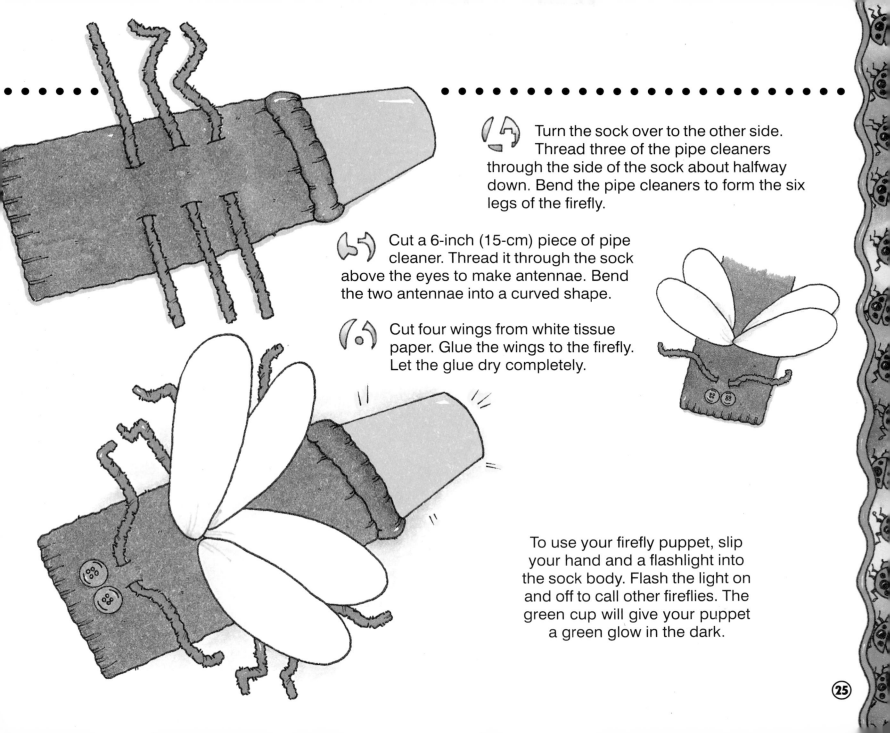

Turn the sock over to the other side. Thread three of the pipe cleaners through the side of the sock about halfway down. Bend the pipe cleaners to form the six legs of the firefly.

Cut a 6-inch (15-cm) piece of pipe cleaner. Thread it through the sock above the eyes to make antennae. Bend the two antennae into a curved shape.

Cut four wings from white tissue paper. Glue the wings to the firefly. Let the glue dry completely.

To use your firefly puppet, slip your hand and a flashlight into the sock body. Flash the light on and off to call other fireflies. The green cup will give your puppet a green glow in the dark.

Queen Wasp and Chambers

Here is what you need:

yellow modeling clay
one straight pin
thin black pipe cleaner
sharp black permanent marker
clear plastic wrap
nine 5-inch (12.5-cm) cardboard tubes
brown poster paint
paintbrush
uncooked rice
white glue
Styrofoam tray for drying

Here is what you do:

1. Glue the sides of the tubes together in pyramid fashion, with four on the bottom, then three on top of those, then two at the top. Let the structure dry on the Styrofoam tray.

2. Paint the tubes brown and let them dry on the tray again. The tubes will be the chambers of the nest.

3. Glue a tiny rice egg in some of the chambers.

Wasps make a nest called a comb. The comb is made up of many little rooms called chambers. The queen wasp lays an egg in each chamber.

26

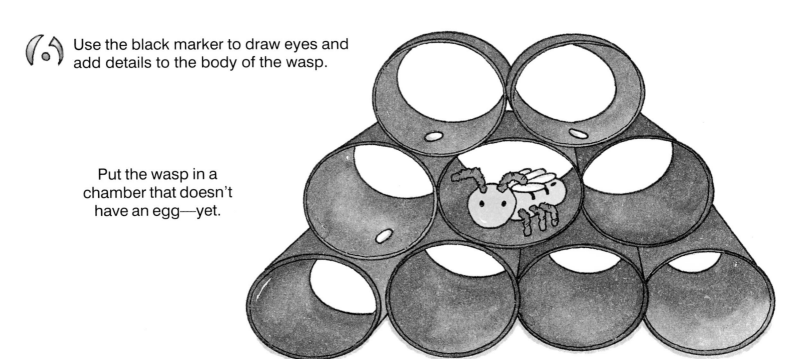

To make the wasp, shape a 2 1/2-inch (6 1/2-cm) body with three segments out of the yellow clay. Cut pieces of black pipe cleaner about 3/4 inch (2 cm) long. Stick three pipe cleaners in each side of the body for legs. Bend the legs down a little. Stick the other two pipe cleaners in the top of the head for the antennae.

Cut two wings from plastic wrap. Use the straight pin to attach the wings to the top of the body.

Use the black marker to draw eyes and add details to the body of the wasp.

Put the wasp in a chamber that doesn't have an egg—yet.

Hungry Mosquito

Here is what you need:

eyedropper
brown pipe cleaner
three hairpins
used white dryer sheet
two tiny wiggle eyes
white glue
scissors
pink sponge
black permanent marker
red food coloring
1/2 cup (125 ml) water
small shallow dish

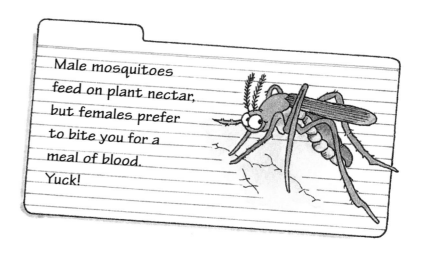

Male mosquitoes feed on plant nectar, but females prefer to bite you for a meal of blood. Yuck!

Here is what you do:

To make the mosquito, wrap the brown pipe cleaner around the tube of the eyedropper, leaving the tip exposed.

Wrap the three hairpins around the body between the pipe cleaners to form the legs. Bend the legs out, then downward, about halfway down each leg. Rub glue over the place where the legs and pipe cleaner touch.

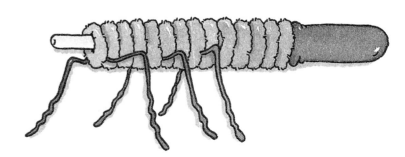

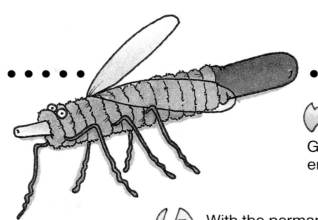

Cut two wings from the dryer sheet. Glue the wings on the back of the mosquito. Glue the two wiggle eyes at the dropper tip end of the mosquito.

With the permanent marker, draw a hand shape on the sponge. Cut the hand out and place it in the shallow dish.

Mix some "blood" for the mosquito by adding a few drops of red food coloring to the 1/2 cup of water. Pour the "blood" on the sponge hand and let it absorb the liquid. Bring the mosquito in for a landing on the hand, bury the dropper nose in the sponge, squeeze the bulb of the eyedropper, and watch the mosquito get a meal.

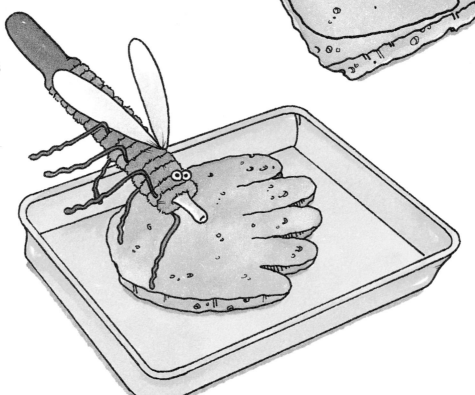

Jumping Grasshopper

Here is what you need:

cardboard egg carton
yellow and green construction paper
black marker
green paint and a paintbrush
1 1/2-inch (3 3/4-cm) rubber ball
two straight pins
scissors
white glue
newspaper to work on

A grasshopper is able to jump about twenty times its own body length. Wow! What if you could do that?

Here is what you do:

Cut a row of three attached cups from the egg carton.

Paint the outside of the cups green and let the paint dry.

Place the ball inside the middle cup. Push a straight pin into the ball through each side of the cup to hold the ball in place.

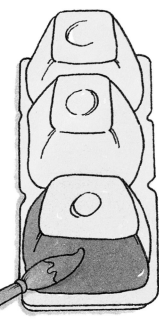

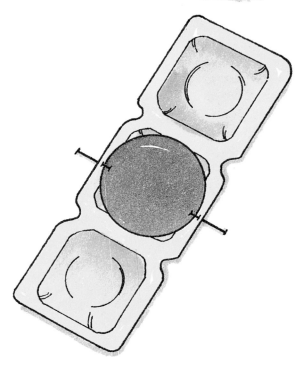

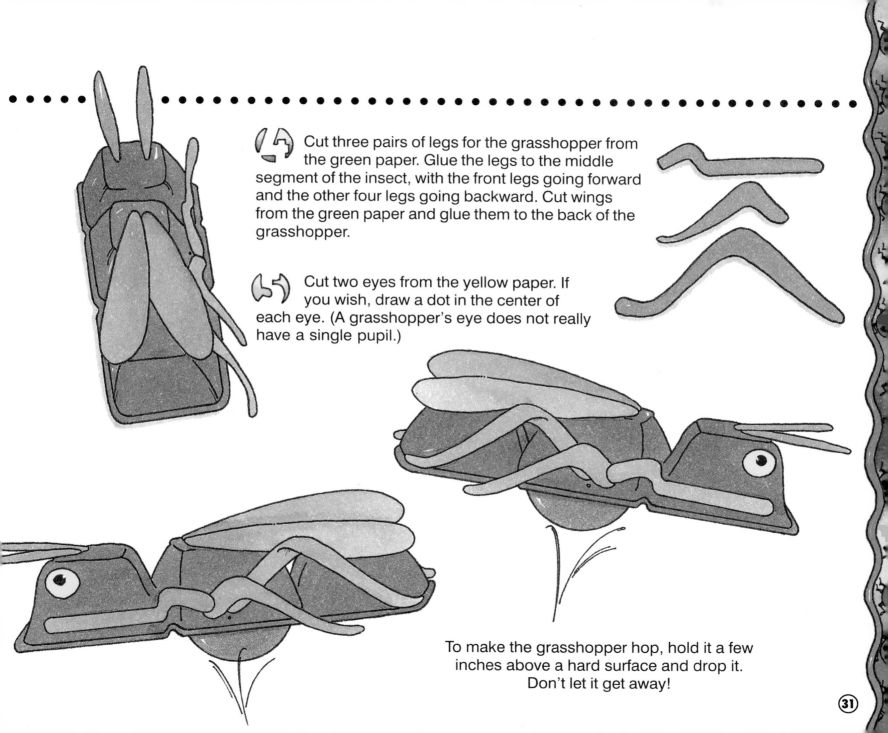

Cut three pairs of legs for the grasshopper from the green paper. Glue the legs to the middle segment of the insect, with the front legs going forward and the other four legs going backward. Cut wings from the green paper and glue them to the back of the grasshopper.

Cut two eyes from the yellow paper. If you wish, draw a dot in the center of each eye. (A grasshopper's eye does not really have a single pupil.)

To make the grasshopper hop, hold it a few inches above a hard surface and drop it. Don't let it get away!

Dog and Flea Game

Here is what you need:

large-size oatmeal box
large brown or black ribbed sock
white, red, and black construction paper scraps
two 1 1/2-inch (3 3/4-cm) black or brown pom-poms
scissors
white glue
brown tissue paper
black marker
one or more 1 1/2-inch (3 3/4-cm) rubber balls

Forty million years ago when a giant woolly mammoth lumbered by, there were fleas waiting to hop on board!

Here is what you do:

Pull the cuff of the brown sock up over the oatmeal box to cover it. Cut the excess sock off at the foot end.

Cut two long, floppy dog ears from the foot of the sock. Glue them on each side of the top of the oatmeal box.

Cut eyes for the dog from the white paper. Add some black pupils, and then glue the eyes near the top front of the box between the ears.

Cut a tongue for the dog from the red paper. Glue it on below the eyes. Glue the two pom-poms above the tongue to shape the dog's muzzle.

To make each flea, cut a piece of brown tissue large enough to cover the ball. Wrap it around the ball and glue the ends together on one side. Trim off the excess tissue. Use the black marker to give the flea a face and legs. Let the glue dry.

Fleas just love to hop onto dogs. Can you hop a flea into the top of the dog you made? Or, try hopping the flea and use the dog container to try to catch it.

Moth and Candle Stabile

Here is what you need:

5-inch (12 1/2-cm) cardboard tube
construction paper
cellophane tape
masking tape
modeling clay
four thin 12-inch (30-cm) black pipe cleaners
white and yellow tissue paper
brown crayon

Moths fly at night and are attracted to light.

Here is what you do:

Roll a ball of clay to fit in one end of the tube for weight. Tape over the opening of the tube with masking tape to hold the clay inside.

To make the candle, cut a piece of construction paper to cover the tube. Tape down the seam of the paper to hold it in place around the tube.

Fold a piece of white tissue paper in half. Cut a double bump shape on the fold, to be opened up to form the wings of a moth. Wrap the end of a black pipe cleaner around the center of the wings, pinching the

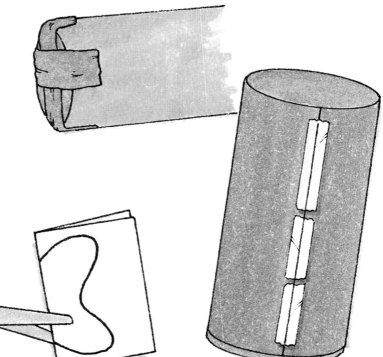

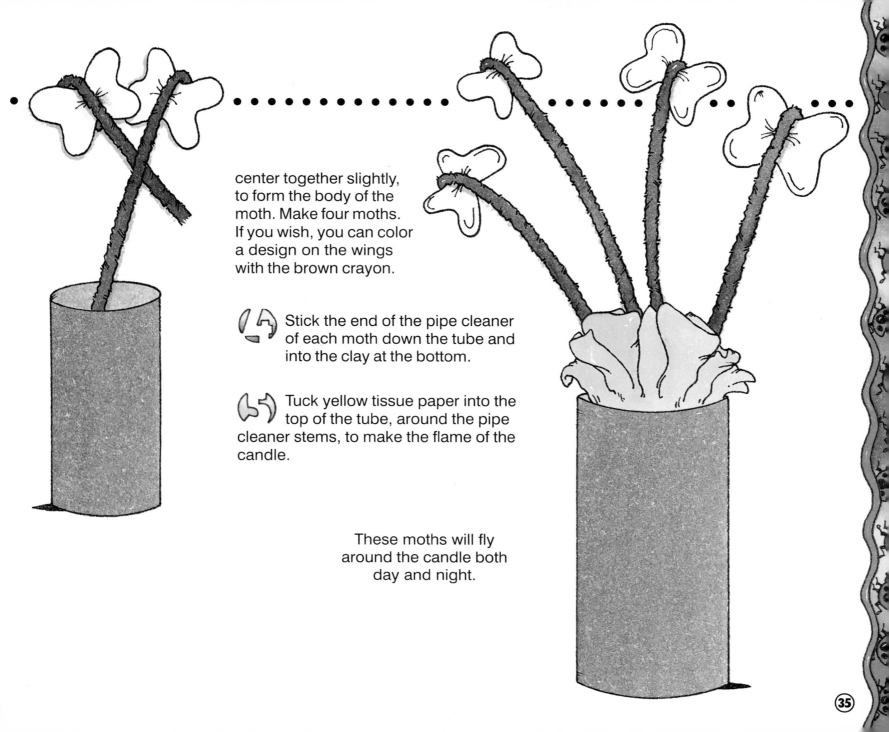

center together slightly, to form the body of the moth. Make four moths. If you wish, you can color a design on the wings with the brown crayon.

Stick the end of the pipe cleaner of each moth down the tube and into the clay at the bottom.

Tuck yellow tissue paper into the top of the tube, around the pipe cleaner stems, to make the flame of the candle.

These moths will fly around the candle both day and night.

Hunting Dragonfly

Here is what you need:

thick green pipe cleaner, 12 inches (30 cm) long
brown pipe cleaner
clear Con-Tact paper
ten tiny wiggle eyes
white thread
green yarn
scissors
pencil
white glue

Dragonflies can fly very fast. Some scientists estimate that they can travel at 60 miles (97 km) an hour.

Here is what you do:

On the paper side of the Con-Tact paper, use the pencil to sketch two wings attached at the center and about 7 inches (18 cm) long. Stack up four pieces of Con-Tact paper and cut out four double wings.

Cut about twenty 6- to 8-inch (15- to 20-cm) pieces of thread. Peel the paper off one of the wings and cover the sticky side with a web of crisscrossed threads. Peel the paper off a second wing piece and stick it directly over the thread-covered wing. Trim the excess threads and Con-Tact paper from around the wings so that the top and bottom pieces match exactly. Then make another set of wings.

Bend the green pipe cleaner in half. Twist the folded end to form a head.

Cut three 2 1/2-inch (6-cm) pieces of brown pipe cleaner for the legs. Slip them between the folded green pipe cleaner just below the head. Slip the two wings in behind the legs. Twist the remainder of the green pipe cleaner to form the long body of the dragonfly and to hold the wings and legs in place. Bend the legs down and forward to form the leg "basket" a dragonfly uses to catch other insects for dinner.

Glue five tiny eyes on each side of the head to represent the compound eyes. A dragonfly actually has 28,000 lenses!

Thread a long piece of green yarn through the pipe cleaner body above the wings of the dragonfly. You can hang the insect from the ceiling or fly it around.

You might want to slip a small plastic bug in
the leg basket of your dragonfly.

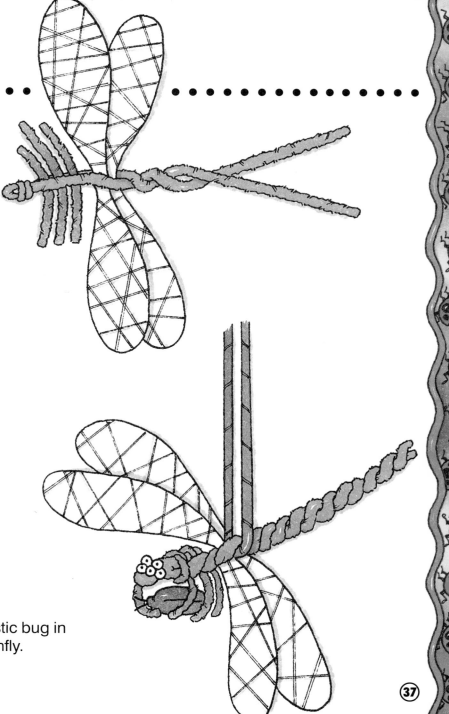

Worker Ant

Here is what you need:

three 2 1/2-inch (6-cm) Styrofoam balls
adult-size black sock
black yarn
four 12-inch (30-cm) black pipe cleaners
two yellow thumbtacks
black permanent marker
piece of white packing Styrofoam
scissors

An ant can lift a weight 50 times as heavy as its own body.

Here is what you do:

Push the three Styrofoam balls into the foot of the black sock so that they are in a row. Push them all the way to the toe of the sock. Tie the opening of the sock shut with a piece of black yarn, as close to the last Styrofoam ball as you can. Trim off the excess sock and the ends of the black yarn.

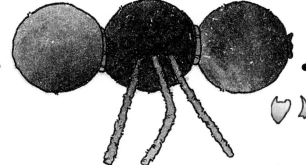

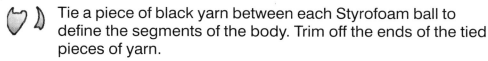

 Tie a piece of black yarn between each Styrofoam ball to define the segments of the body. Trim off the ends of the tied pieces of yarn.

Cut three of the 12-inch-long black pipe cleaners in half so that you have six 6-inch (15-cm) pieces. Push three pieces into each side of the middle segment of the ant to make the legs. Bend each leg down in the middle.

Break off a 1-inch (2 1/2-cm) piece of packing Styrofoam to make a sugar grain for the ant to carry. Push the end of each front leg into each side of the Styrofoam so that the ant is holding the grain.

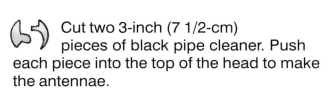

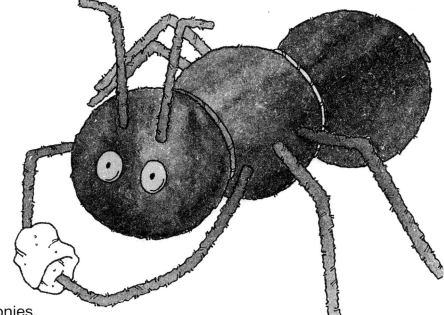

Cut two 3-inch (7 1/2-cm) pieces of black pipe cleaner. Push each piece into the top of the head to make the antennae.

Push the two yellow thumbtacks into the front of the head to make the eyes. Use the black marker to draw a dot in the center of each tack.

Ants live together in big colonies. Maybe you should make lots of ants!

Ants on a Picnic Basket Necklace

Here is what you need:

yellow plastic twist-off bottle cap
yellow pipe cleaner
pretty fabric scrap
fruit-shaped candies
black peppercorns
green yarn
scissors
white glue

When one ant discovers food, it goes to find its friends, leaving a scent trail for them to follow back to the goodies.

Here is what you do:

To make the basket, cover the inside of the bottle cap with glue. Cut a 2-inch (5-cm) square of fabric and tuck it into the basket, print side down.

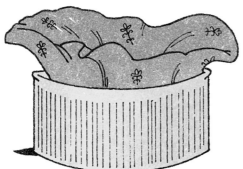

Glue three fruit-shaped candies in the basket. Squeeze glue over the tops of the candies and fold the edges of the fabric up and over the candies, tucking the edges between them so that they stick out from the fabric.

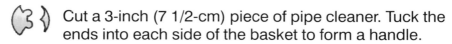 Cut a 3-inch (7 1/2-cm) piece of pipe cleaner. Tuck the ends into each side of the basket to form a handle.

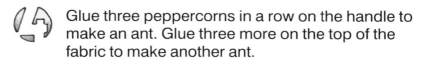 Glue three peppercorns in a row on the handle to make an ant. Glue three more on the top of the fabric to make another ant.

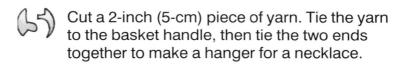 Cut a 2-inch (5-cm) piece of yarn. Tie the yarn to the basket handle, then tie the two ends together to make a hanger for a necklace.

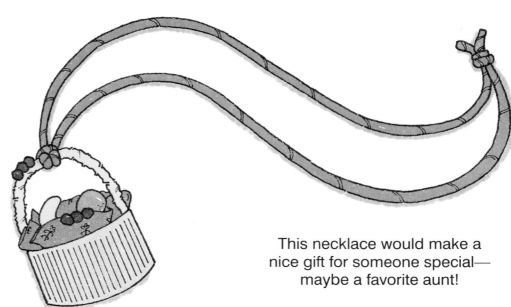

This necklace would make a nice gift for someone special— maybe a favorite aunt!

Venus's Flytrap and Fly Puppets

Here is what you need:

two white cotton work gloves
orange felt
adult-size brown sock
green poster paint
paintbrush
scissors
white glue
black glove
white dryer sheet
two tiny wiggle eyes
Styrofoam tray for drying

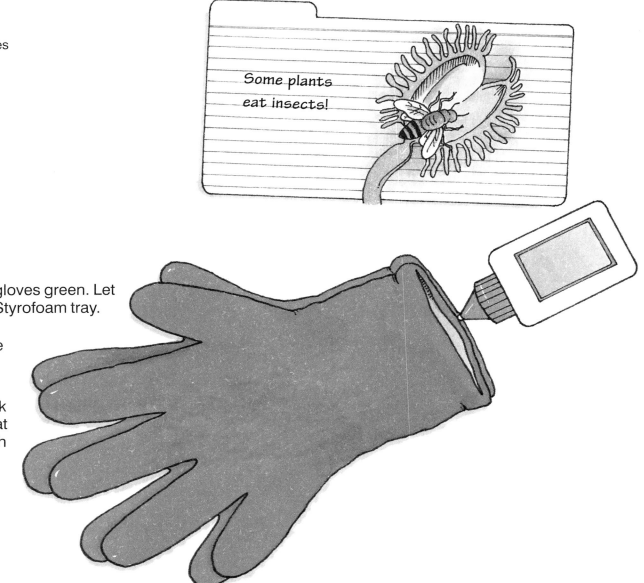

Some plants eat insects!

Here is what you do:

Paint both work gloves green. Let them dry on the Styrofoam tray.

Cut the toe off the brown sock.

Glue the two work gloves together at the bottom cuff only, with the palms facing in.

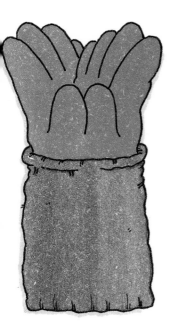

Rub glue around the outside of the two gloves up to the fingers, then pull the cut end of the sock up around the two gloves to form the stem of the plant.

Cut two 3-inch (7 1/2-cm) square pieces of felt. Glue them down in between the two gloves to form the inner lining of the plant.

To make the fly, cut a finger off the black glove. Glue two wiggle eyes at the tip of the finger. Cut wings from the dryer sheet and glue them on the finger behind the eyes.

To use your Venus's-flytrap puppet, slip your hand into one glove of the plant. Put the fly on a finger of your other hand. When the fly touches the sensitive plant, snap your hand shut and your plant will have its dinner.

Scurrying Cockroach

Here is what you need:

tiny toy car about 1 1/2 to 2 inches
    (3 3/4 to 5 cm) long
black and brown felt
white glue
plastic cup
craft stick
rubber band
scissors
water
two tiny wiggle eyes
thin wire
masking tape
Styrofoam tray for drying

Roaches have been around since before the dinosaurs.

Here is what you do:

 Cover the top and sides of the car with masking tape to create a better gluing surface.

Cut a piece of black felt large enough to cover the top and sides of the car.

Mix about 1/2 cup (125 ml) of glue with a few drops of water in the cup. Use the craft stick to stir the mixture well.

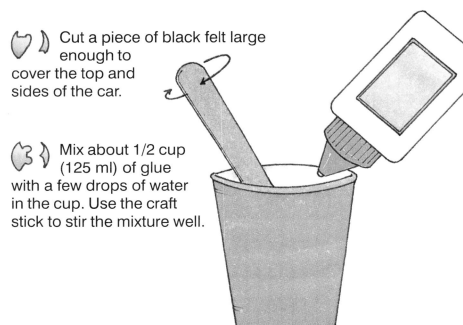

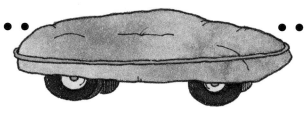

Working on the Styrofoam tray, put the felt in the watery glue and mix it around until it is totally covered with glue on both sides. Squeeze the excess glue out of the felt and shape it over the top and sides of the car. Hold the felt in place over the car with the rubber band.

Trim off the extra felt around the bottom of the car.

Let the car dry completely on a Styrofoam tray. When it is dry, remove the rubber band.

Bend a piece of wire in half to make two 2-inch (5-cm) antennae for the roach. Cut a small head from brown felt. Tape the antennae to the underside of the head, then glue the head to one end of the roach body. Curve the two wire antennae out and slightly around.

Glue two tiny wiggle eyes to the front of the insect.

When the glue has dried, the roach will be ready to scurry across your kitchen floor.

Bug in the Grass Terrarium

Here is what you need:

two clear disposable plastic cups
1-inch (2 1/2-cm) round stone
a few pebbles
potting soil
grass seed
water
cellophane tape
nail polish in one or more colors
sharp black permanent marker

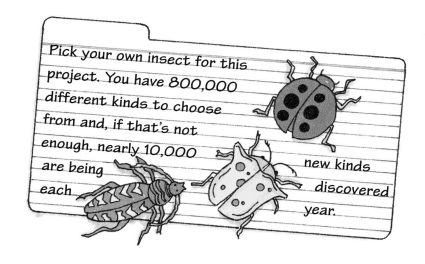

Pick your own insect for this project. You have 800,000 different kinds to choose from and, if that's not enough, nearly 10,000 new kinds are being discovered each year.

Here is what you do:

To make a bug for your terrarium, paint the stone with nail polish and let it dry. Add details to the bug with a permanent marker.

Put a few pebbles in the bottom of one cup. Fill the cup about 3/4 full with potting soil.

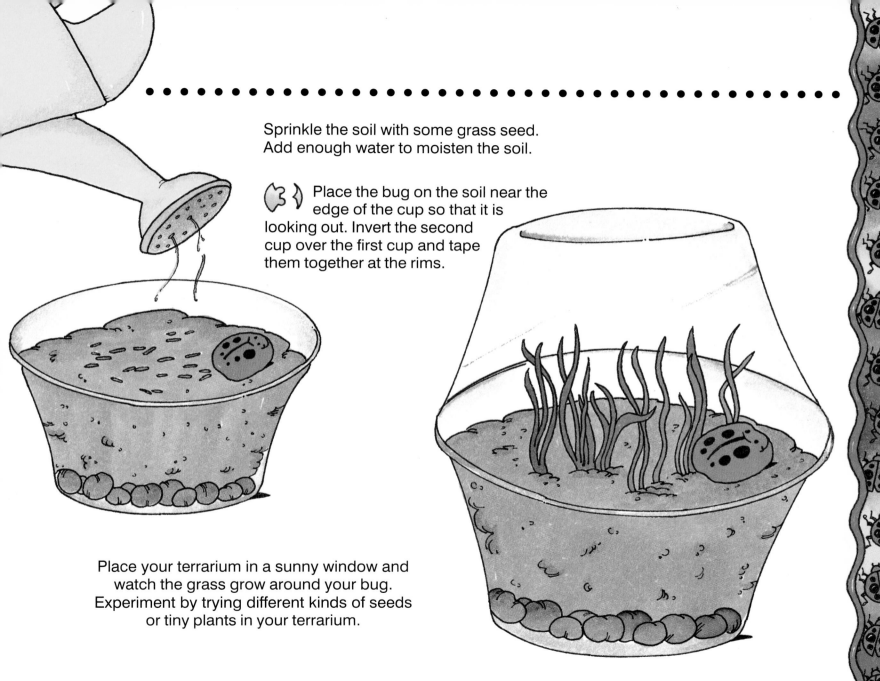

Sprinkle the soil with some grass seed. Add enough water to moisten the soil.

Place the bug on the soil near the edge of the cup so that it is looking out. Invert the second cup over the first cup and tape them together at the rims.

Place your terrarium in a sunny window and watch the grass grow around your bug. Experiment by trying different kinds of seeds or tiny plants in your terrarium.

Books About Insects

Bourgoing, Pascale de. *The Ladybug and Other Insects.* New York: Scholastic, 1991.

Facklam, Margery. *The Big Bug Book.* Boston: Little, Brown, 1993.

Gaffney, Michael. *Secret Forests.* Racine, WI: Golden Books, 1994.

Insects. New York: Dorling Kindersley, 1992.

Kalman, Bobbie. *Bugs and Other Insects.* New York: Crabtree, 1994.

Macquitty, Miranda. *Amazing Bugs.* New York: Dorling Kindersley, 1996.

McGavin, George. *Insects of North America.* San Diego: Thunder Bay Press, 1995.

Mound, L.A. *Insects.* New York: Dorling Kindersley, 1995.

Parker, Jane. *Focus on Insects.* London: Gloucester Press, 1993.

Parker, Nancy Winslow. *Bugs.* New York: Greenwillow Books, 1987.

Parker, Steve. *Beastly Bugs.* Austin, TX: Raintree Steck-Vaughn, 1994.

Richardson, Joy. *Insects.* New York: Franklin Watts, 1993.

Russo, Monica. *The Insect Almanac.* New York: Sterling, 1991.

Wechsler, Doug. *Bizarre Bugs.* New York: Cobblehill Books, 1995.

Woelflein, Luise. *The Ultimate Bug Book.* New York: Western, 1993.

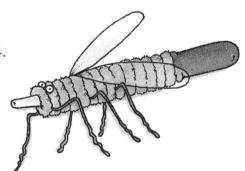